Ravi
the Ray

Written by Gloria Barnett

Illustrated by Pam Clubb

Footprint to the Future

Ravi the ray is a flat-shaped fish with a beautiful blue-spotted pattern on his back. He lay on the seabed, covered by a light dusting of sand.

PHEW! He was exhausted after a busy night hunting for food.

Warm sunlight shone down through the shimmering ocean water above him and warmed his back. It was calm and peaceful.

He tried to keep his eyes open,
but slowly he fell asleep.

Suddenly, the water around him began to
move and swirl. He opened his eyes and
looked around.

A diver with a camera was swimming nearby.

flash! flash! flash!
flash! flash! flash
flash! flash! flash

flash! flash! flash! flash! flash! flash! flash! flash! flash! flash! flash! flash! flash!

The sudden light from the camera frightened him.

Ravi pushed himself upwards and swiftly swam to the other side of the coral reef.

He settled down in the sand, closed his eyes and relaxed.

But not for long!

Something moved across his skin.
Something gooey, sticky and slimy.

GLOOP! GLOOP! GLOOP! GLOOP!

Oh, sea slug!

I know you're beautiful and can't hurt me, but I don't like you crawling all over me with your sticky mess.

Ravi shivered and shook his body until the tiny sea slug fell off his back.

Something tickled his skin.
Arrgh! What was that?

Oh, it's you, baby octopus. Are you using your tentacles to tickle me?
Please leave me alone, I'd like to go to sleep
Sorry, I thought you'd like to play.

Ravi set off to find a quieter place.

Why do I always have to look for somewhere peaceful to go to sleep?

He saw a hole under the coral reef and carefully swam inside.
The hole was the perfect size for Ravi.
He felt cosy, warm and safe.

He'd just closed his eyes when he felt the water moving again.

He glanced upwards and saw some tiny Nemo fish. They were playing tag and going in and out of the finger-like tentacles of an anemone coral.

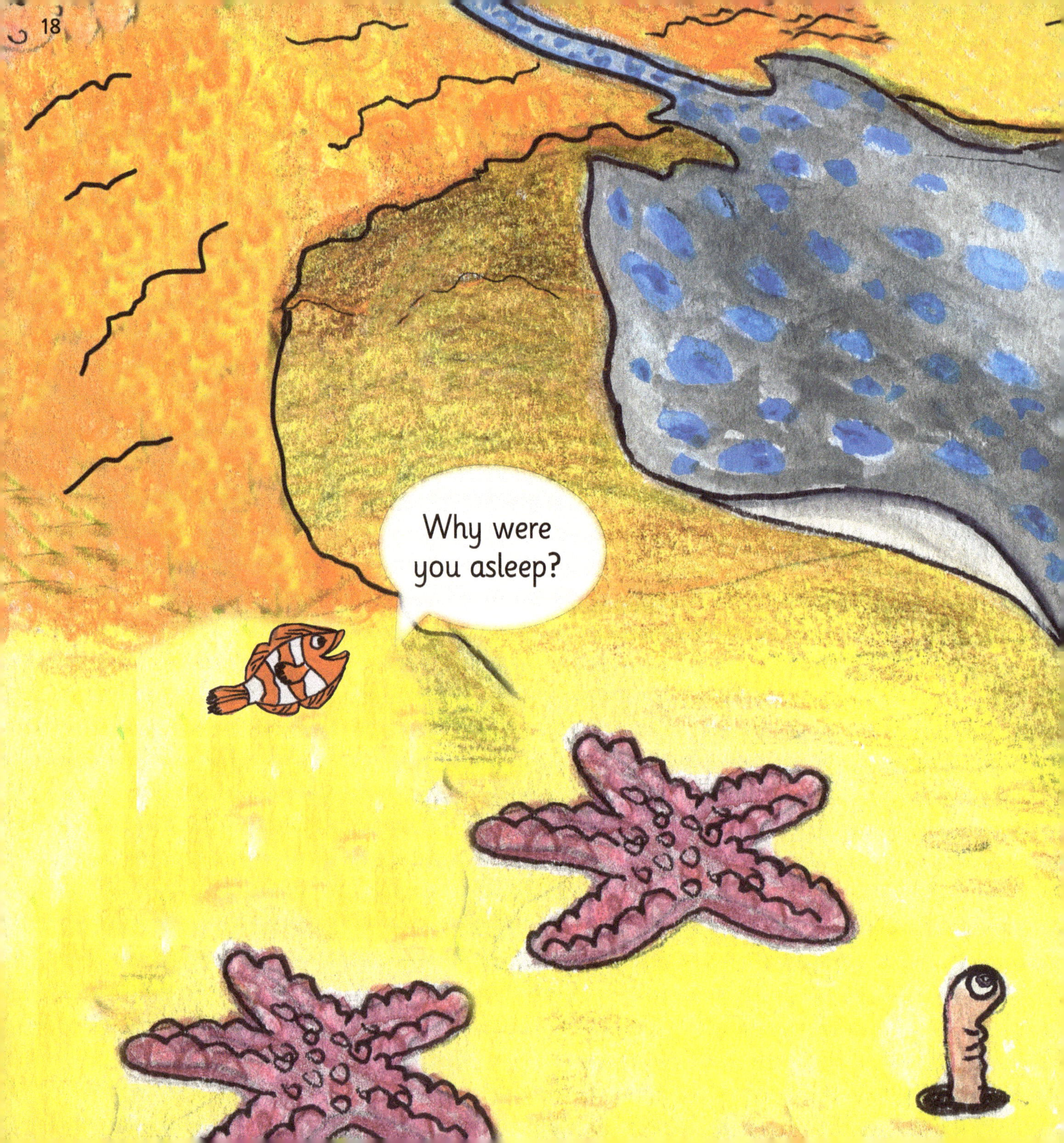
Why were you asleep?

I swim around at night-time hunting for food.

But it's difficult to sleep when there's so much going on around me all day.

Yes. All our family live inside the tentacles of this anemone coral. It keeps us safe.

Where is your family?

I don't know.

When I was born, I only remember popping out from an egg case and starting to swim around.

I've always been alone, and I've never had a home of my own.

Our anemone coral is a wonderful home. We're all so safe inside there.

I love snuggling in-between the tentacles where the big fish can't see me.

Why don't you settle down for
your daytime sleep?

I'll ask my brothers and sisters to
leave you in peace for a while.

Perhaps we can chat with you later?
We can all be friends, can't we?

When Ravi woke up, he saw it was getting dark.
The day was turning to night.
He felt hungry.
It was time to hunt for food.

A tiny sand eel darted out in front of him.
He gulped it down in one quick mouthful.
He kept his eyes looking around for any dangerous creature
who might want to eat him.

He searched the watery darkness all night, feeding until he was
no longer hungry.
Life was good.

Then daylight began to shine down from the surface of the sea.
Ravi turned to swim back to his new home beneath the
anemone coral.

As he moved through the water, Ravi became aware of something following him.

He turned to look.

A VERY LARGE FISH

was coming his way.

He needed to get back to the safety of the anemone coral.

He swam **faster** and **faster**.

The large fish was getting **closer** and **closer**.

He could see the coral, ahead of him.
He could see the little Nemo fish jumping up and down.
He could hear them cheering him on.
He could see the space ... his safe space.

But he had never practised sliding into his small space beneath the coral, and he definitely hadn't practised sliding in at SPEED!

He needed to be FAST enough NOT be caught by the big fish but SLOW enough NOT to crash into the hard, scratchy coral rocks. Could he do it?

It was going to be very tricky.

WHOOSH!

Ravi shot towards the space beneath the coral, but he was out of control.

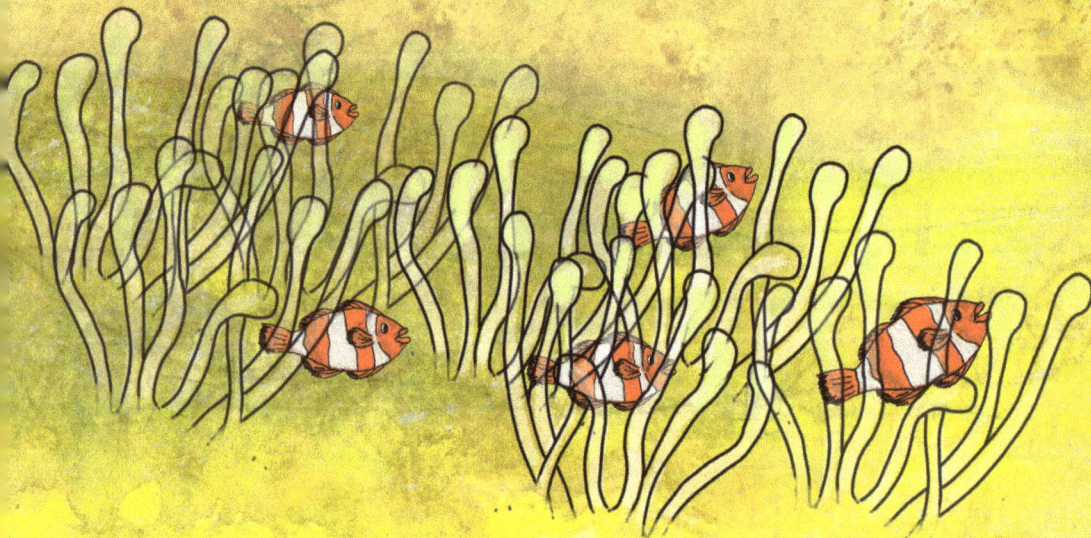

TWIRL! He was spinning around and went sliding downwards into the sand.

The sand particles swirled around him like a large cloud.

BANG!

His nose crunched into the hard, rocky coral. He lay still. He could see stars circling above his throbbing head.

But he'd arrived and was safe.

Ouch! I'm going to have a MASSIVE headache later, he thought.

All Ravi's little Nemo friends came out of
the anemone to see what was happening.

At first, they looked worried, but they were
soon laughing and chattering.

Are you alright?

I was cheering you on as you
came towards us.

It was so exciting to watch.

That BIG fish was coming up
very fast behind you.

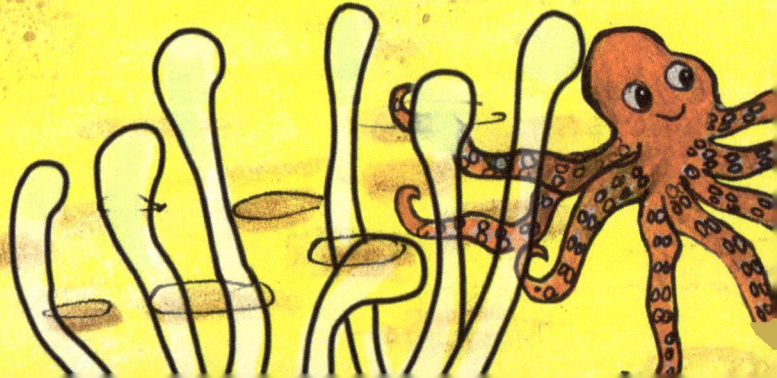

Your nose looks a bit bent!
Phew, that entry was a bit toooooooo….. fast.
We're so pleased you came back.

We're all so happy you're living here with us now!

It's great to be here.

You're all so kind, it feels like I'm part of your family now.

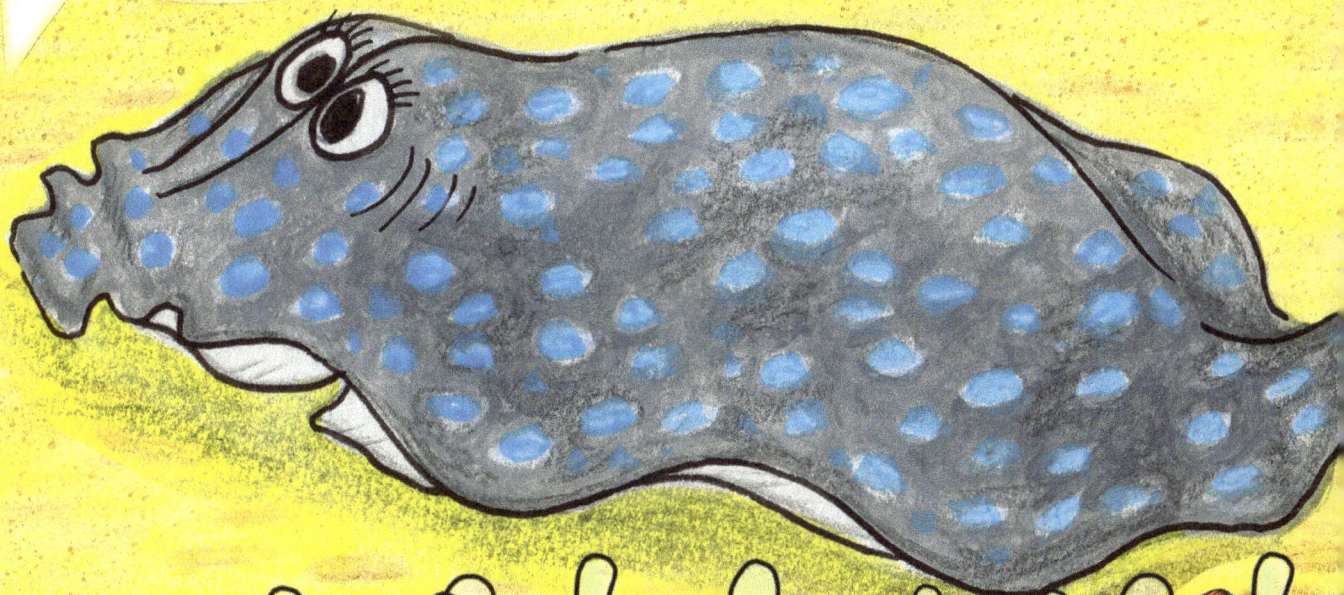

Ravi popped his head out of his space and looked around for the big fish.

He saw it swimming, far away in the distance. The danger was over!

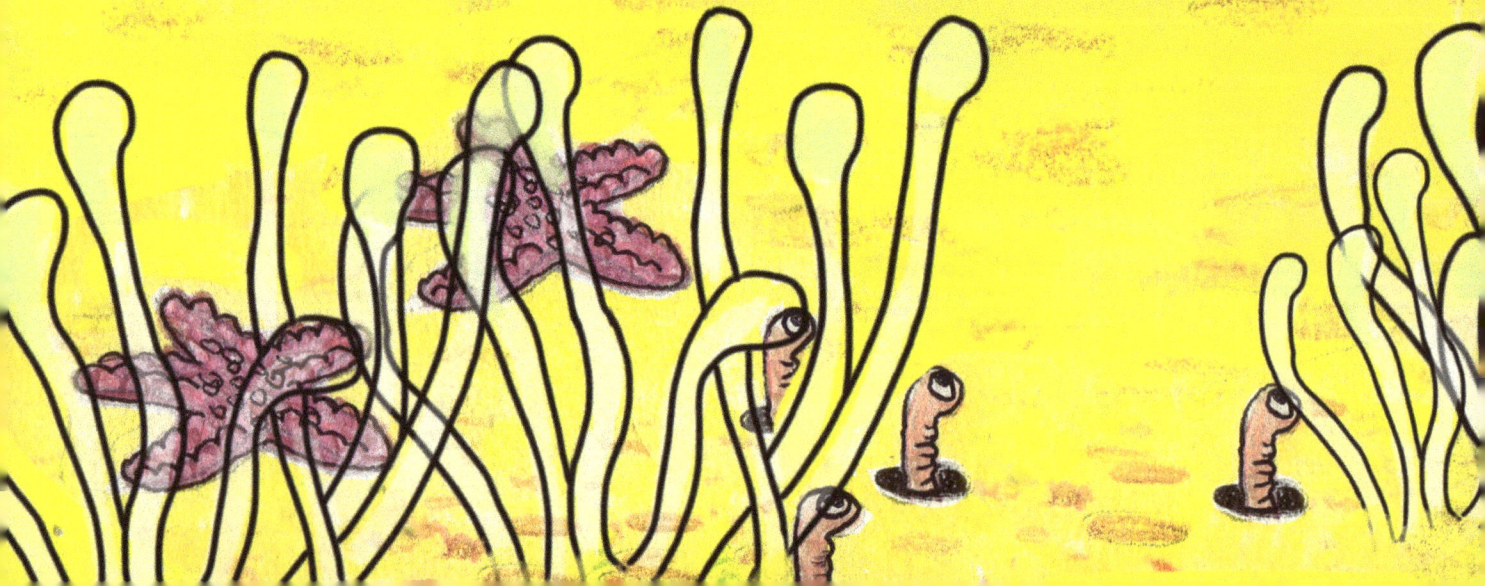

Ravi still had to avoid slimy sea slugs and dangerous creatures when he went hunting for food, but ...

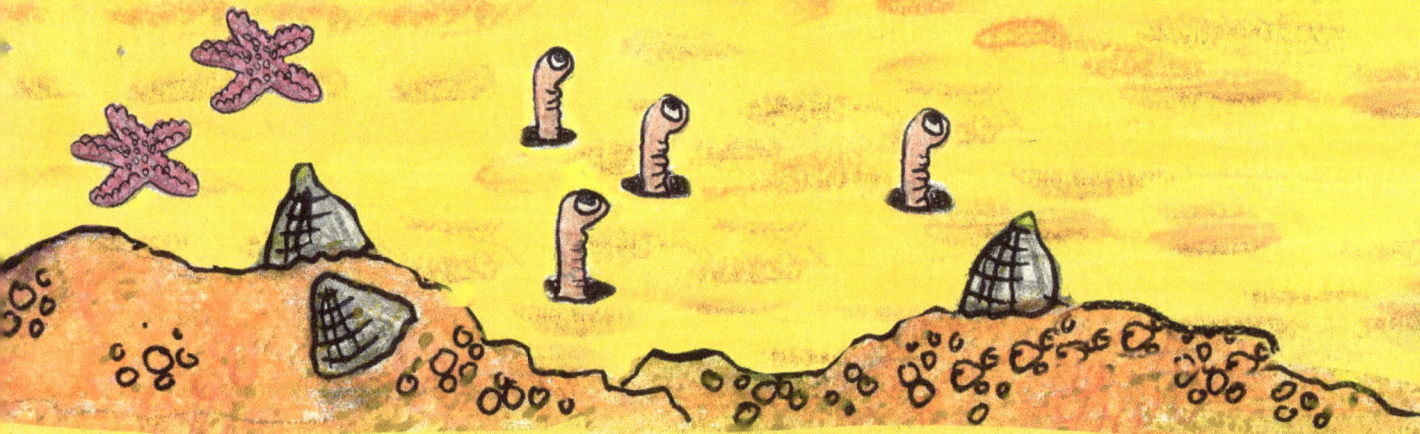

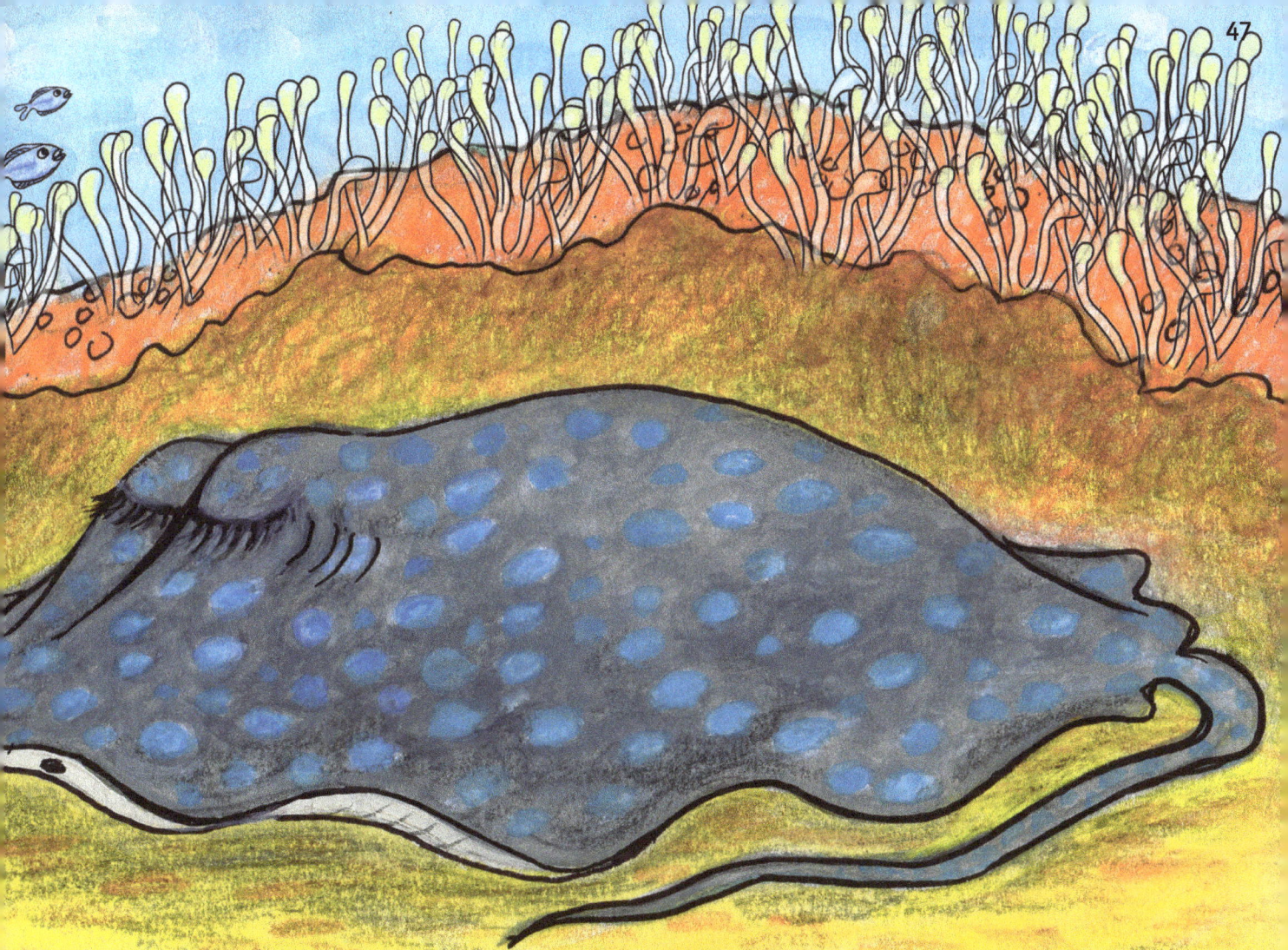

NOW... he had friends.

NOW... he had somewhere where he could lay his head and sleep safely every day.

It felt good to be home.

Sleep well Ravi.

SCIENCE STUFF ... DID YOU KNOW?
NEMO FISH AND ANEMONE CORAL

- *Nemo fish* get their name from the fact that they live inside ANEMONE coral. They are also called clownfish because they are as colourful as clowns.

- Nemo fish live on coral reefs in the ocean and eat tiny shrimps and plankton.

- Nemo fish are the only fish that can live inside *anemone* corals.

- The anemone coral has poisonous tentacles which stop fish from eating them, but Nemo fish produce a special protective gel over their bodies and the gel allows Nemo fish to go inside the anemone coral without being stung.

- The anemone coral and the Nemo fish live happily together – helping each other to stay safe. Nemo fish can hide in the coral tentacles and bring up their families whilst the Nemo fish frighten away other fish from coming too close, so the anemone coral is protected from being eaten.

SCIENCE STUFF ... DID YOU KNOW?
BLUE SPOTTED RAYS

- There are many different species of Ray, including Blue–Spotted Rays, Stingrays, Eagle Rays, Electric Rays and Manta Rays.

- They have large, flat fins that are rounded and stretch along the sides of their bodies. The ray uses a rippling movement like a wave, to move through the water. The movement makes it look like the ray is flying.

- They are 'bottom feeders' and have a mouth under their head that searches the sandy seabed for food.

- Rays are cousins of sharks. Both sharks and rays have skeletons made of cartilage rather than bones to support their bodies.

- Blue-spotted rays have a tail with one or two spines that contain poison. The sting from a spine is very painful, so it's best to keep away from them.

- Rays give birth to live young, but they don't live together as families. Once born, a ray leads a solitary life.

- Rays have prominent eyes which stand up from their head.

- Blue-spotted rays can grow up to 80 cm in length and weigh up to 5kg.

OTHER TITLES BY THIS AUTHOR:

FISHY TALE STORYBOOKS
AGE 3-6

A FISHY TALES STORYBOOK

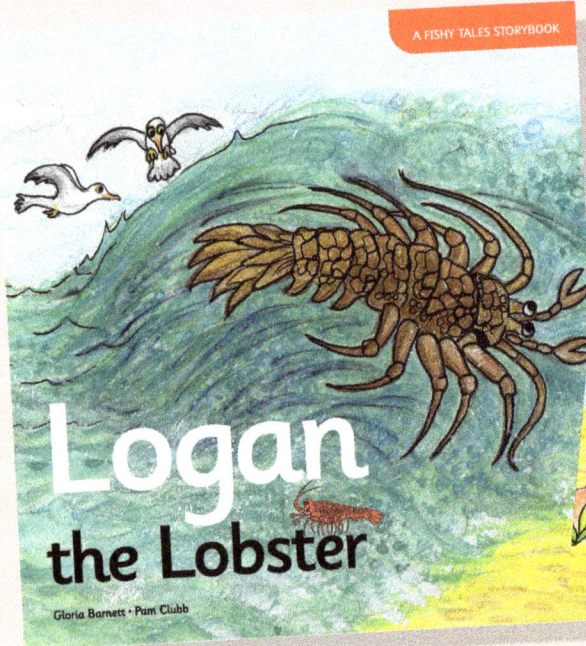

**Logan
the Lobster**

Gloria Barnett · Pam Clubb

A FISHY TALES STORYBOOK

**Prickle
the Puffer Fish**

Gloria Barnett · Pam Clubb

This way to Puffer Fish school

Logan the Lobster

Logan was different from all the other little lobsters. Would they be his friends? Would they play with him?

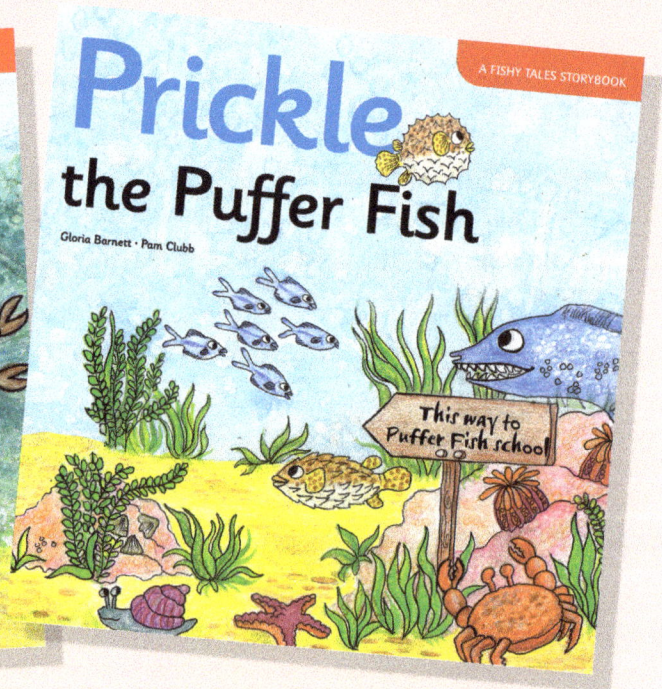

Prickle the Puffer Fish

A coral reef can be a very dangerous place to live. How can Prickle keep herself safe? Can she be brave?

OTHER TITLES BY THIS AUTHOR:

LUCY'S ADVENTURES
AGE 8-12

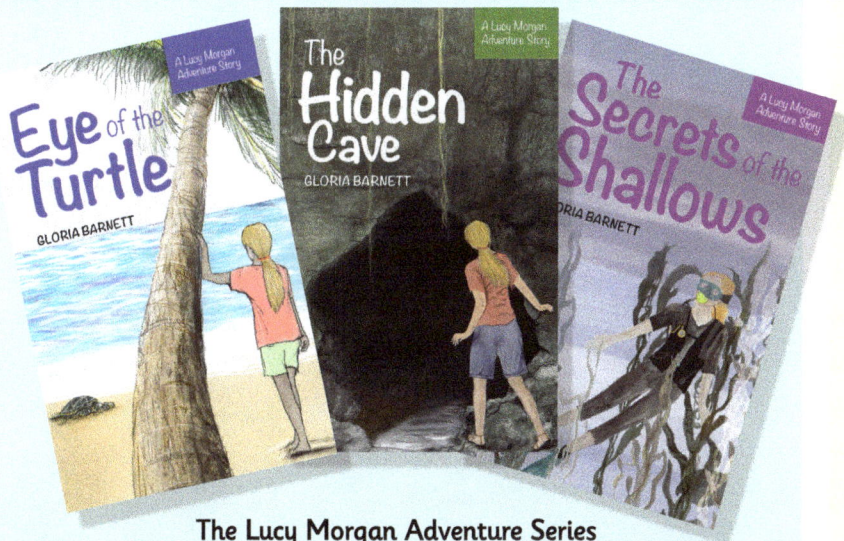

The Lucy Morgan Adventure Series

Lucy loves oceans and the creatures which live there. She promises to help to protect them but there are challenges ahead in the underwater world. Can Lucy make a difference to life in the oceans and help protect our planet?

A GUIDE TO OCEANS
AGE 10-110

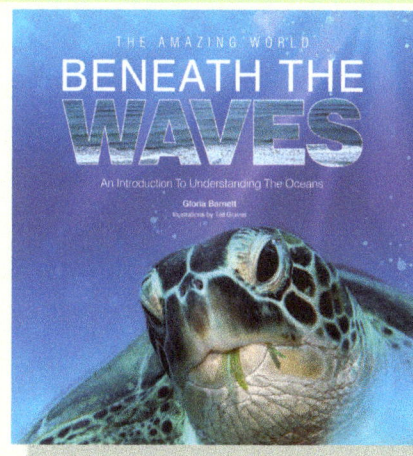

The Amazing World Beneath the Waves

Review: 'A tremendous subject presented in a clear and concise way.'

50 FABULOUS FACTS
FOR CHILDREN OR ADULTS

This non-fiction book will introduce some of the weird and wonderful species of life in the oceans.

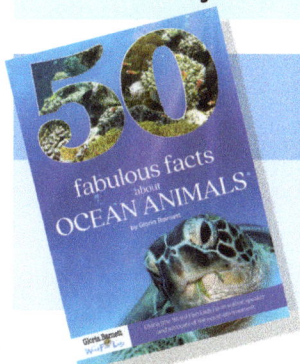

Gloria Barnett
The Weird Fish Lady

More information at:
www.barnettauthor.co.uk

For Ben, Keira and Xander

Published in 2022

An imprint from Footprint to the Future,
165 London Road, Temple Ewell, Kent, CT16 3DA

Text © Gloria Barnett

Illustrations © Pam Clubb

A CIP record for this title is available from the British Library.

ISBN: 978-1-838064358
Book Design: www.amberdesigns.com